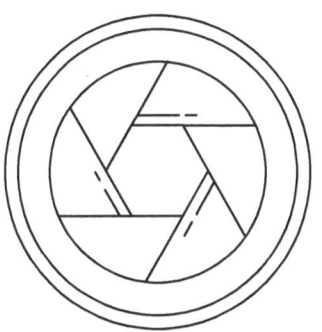

Penile Photography
An Authoritative Handbook

Sebastian T. Armstrong

Introduction

Let's get one thing out of the way: Penile Photography is Art. Taken seriously and elevated to the artistic level it deserves, penile photography is so much more than the hastily taken photographs, quickly published to social media and an un-suspecting, uninterested viewer. While so-called "dick pics", (vulgar slang for penis photographs) have become a ubiquitous, yet unwelcome element in modern culture, photographically it is none-theless trite and banal. The penis is a beautiful organ, symbolically intriguing, func-tionally dynamic and full of meaning to its owner. The personal artistic endeav-or of photographing one's own penis is a journey of self-discovery, a liberation from notions of inadequacies and ultimately an expression of personal creativity and healthy self-love.

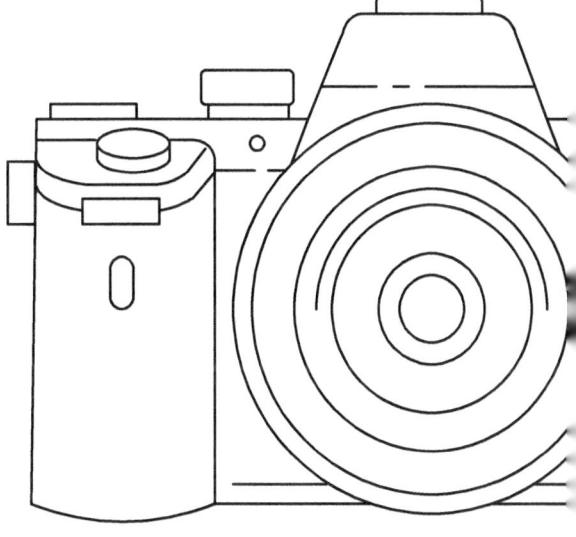

This book will inspire and help you elevate your plain and uninspiring penis photos to beautiful penile art that is appreci-ated on a multitude of levels.

Chapter 1

Cameras – from Smartphone to Pro Equipment

One of the most widely spread misconceptions about photography is that you need professional equipment to create visually pleasing images. And that you need professional gear to take high quality penile photographs. In reality, nothing could be further from the truth. If you know what you are doing, allocate plenty of time and have endurance, even the simplest of smartphones, and most basic point-and-shoot cameras can create powerful penile imagery that inspire viewers. Considering the ongoing technical improvements being made within the realm of photography, including, but certainly not limited to computational photography, there has arguably never been a better time for serious penile photographers.

Even many of today's mid-range smartphones offer multiple optical choices, including, wide angle, telephoto and portrait lens options. Each of these lenses have their advantages and disadvantages. And with each new iteration, phone cameras – both the software and hardware inside them – improve tremendously. The optical quality upgrades approximately every year, and even large leaps are achieved in the field of digital image signal processing and sensor technology.

Sensors in most smartphones are physically small and have a relatively narrow dynamic range, focus options and color gamut. Using artificial intelligence (AI), and machine learning (ML), many limitations of the optics, and the physics involved, can be compensated with software. With recent camera and imaging software implementations, you can produce a series of vibrantly colored, artistically visionary and visually compelling – even enviable – photographs of your penis.

All image sensors, size notwithstanding, capture and record what the camera's lens sees as pixels. The larger the sensor, the bigger the pixels and vice versa. The bigger the pixels, the more image information can theoretically be registered on the sensor. Larger sensors (with larger pixels) usually provide images with higher dynamic range, more options for depth of field and therefore more flexibility during post processing. Today, the camera industries largest sensors are found in so-called *medium format* cameras. The smallest sensors are typically found in smartphones and other mobile image capturing devices, including miniaturized surveillance cameras.

The challenge of all photography – especially penile photography – is in the creative use of the infinite amount of options available. Obviously your range of options depend on budget, technical prowess, creative vision and, ultimately, on the aesthetics of your penis. The beauty and magic lies fundamentally in how you creatively use all available options. With patience, ingenuity and determination, even the most inexpensive and unsophisticated camera can suffice.

Regardless of what kind of camera, lens, or lighting setup you decide to choose, keep in mind that even the slightest angle change, adjustment of focal length and distance, choice of height or background, will ultimately alter your viewers perspective and will influence emotional reaction and connection to your penis.

Zoom In vs Zoom Out

A zoom lens will allow for quick shifts in focal length and vantage point which can help you meet even the most challenging creative ambition. When using a zoom lens, I recommend first experimenting using a simple replacement, or, stand-in. I suggest using two full-sized, shelled walnuts, a bowl of freshly rinsed and air-dried alfalfa sprouts and a straight or slightly curved carrot or zucchini (depending on your preference of color, girth, and texture) as a still life stand-in when composing, adjusting and fixating the focal length, angle, and depth of field. Bear in mind that generally, zoom lenses are heavy and cumbersome to carry and use. Also, less expensive zoom lenses tend to have slower autofocus, limited focal options and lack image stabilization.

Focal Length and Depth of Field

Using a telephoto or zoom lens will give you the freedom to optically 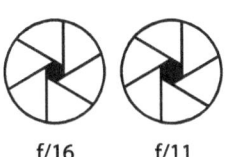 manipulate – enlarge or reduce – the appearance of your penis, including circumference, length and density of pubic hair. This option will perhaps provide you with the most flexibility, but can also effectively give you too many choices and take much more time than expected. Particularly if you are aiming for size enhancement and manipulating proportions rather than simply trying to produce an aesthetically pleasing, artistically composed photograph of your penis.

f/16   f/11

A higher quality zoom lens will allow you to photograph with a so-called "shallow depth of field". This means, for example, if you are shooting downwards from above the waist, that you can have your penis in perfect focus while allowing your scrotum to be somewhat blurred (but not totally distorted and thrown out of context) in the

background. Depending on lighting conditions, a professional grade lens will allow you to choose the level of blurriness, from creamy soft to just slightly out of focus. Often, but not always, many cameras are sold with a telephoto and zoom lens included in the purchase. With a few exceptions, most of these "kit lenses" are not of very high quality – other than during perfect lighting situations and optimal weather conditions. These lenses are often made of plastic, consist of cheap mechani-cal inner workings, and the outer optics (at both ends of the lens's

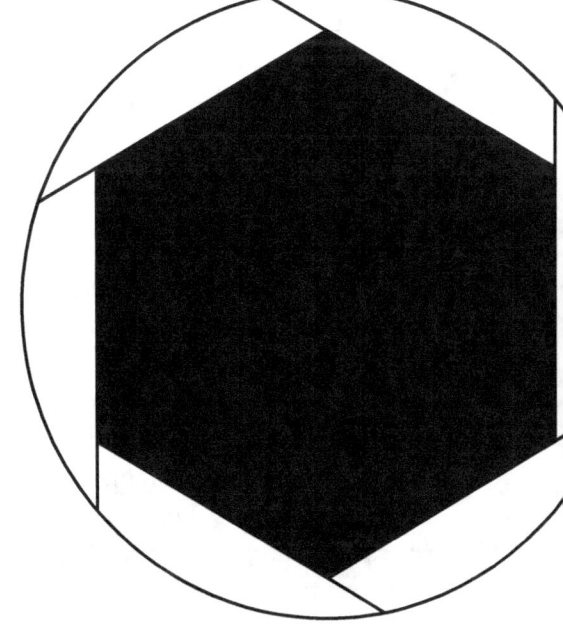

casing) do not have as much protective coating as higher end variants and are therefore easily scratched and damaged.

– I often find that imposing challenging lighting time constraints and technical limitations will often produce more interesting results. Conversely, the more elaborate the setup, the wider the possibilities, albeit the more technically complicated your penile photography session may become.

Macro Photography: Getting Really Close

Getting really closeup shots of your penis can easily be achieved by using a lens that is purpose-built for this type of photography or has a macro setting. Getting closeup images of your penis will consequently put a great deal of demand on the camera position, lighting and composition you choose. For example, focusing on the very tip of the glans head can also reveal or present (depending on your aesthetic preference), exaggerated views of blemishes, scars and veins. On the other hand, a macro lens can also provide excellent opportunities to compel viewers to be visually immersed on a special aspect of the penis, scrotum or manscaped region you feel extraordinarily proud of or find noteworthy. Though somewhat off-topic and technically demanding, a macro lens can also be gainfully used when photographing your anus. The anus is an often neglected erogenous zone. With proper grooming, lighting, and composition, the elastic, wrinkly nature of the anus can incontestably compliment and add creative variety to your penile photography.

Tabletop Tripods

If you are serious about penile photography, and unless you are handy enough to design and create one yourself, you will inevitably need to invest in a tripod. Why? Well, to photograph your penis in a more professional way, you will need to use a relatively long exposure time. Long exposures, at say, 1/15th or 1/5th of a second to compensate for less than optimal lighting conditions, inescapably means there is a profound risk that blurriness through shakes and vibrations are introduced to the capture. Though much can be accomplished with natural lighting, setting a high light sensitivity value (higher ISO), using a camera with a flash or a continuous light (LED) mounted on it or placed nearby, I've found that using a tripod, even a simple model, offers the best support in most circumstances.

Your choice of camera, large, medium or small, will ultimately determine which tripod to choose. Like with much of today's camera gear, the amount of available options offer tremendous width and breadth. From the ultra lightweight carbon fiber to the compact pocket tripods – and everything in between. One serious area to consider is variability. Where one tripod might suit your needs perfectly in an indoor situation with controllable conditions, that same piece of equipment might not suffice when you decide to take your penile photography outdoors or into a more public setting. I suggest purchasing a foldable tabletop tripod, and one that will offer you as more creative latitude as your photographic enthusiasm increases. I always try to buy for the future, not for the present. Like me, one day you too will find the art of penile photography so compelling that you will want to up your game and invest deeper into the genre, both creatively and technically. Gear that allows you to grow in the future will serve as a creative incentive today.

The reverse can of course act oppositely, opting for less expensive photographic tools today, can lead to frustration and technically limit your ability to capture your penis according to your vision and quality demands.

There are many variations of smartphone tripods on the market, some even tiny enough to fit in your wallet. For full-sized camera bodies, including DSLR, mirrorless and medium format, interchangeable lens cameras, you must take into account that these devices add additional weight and stabilization requirements to your tripod. From my own experience where poor judgement and bad luck can at times both play a part, I can assure you that the last thing you want to happen is for your tripod mounted camera to come tumbling down and be destroyed.

Consider also that a quality tripod will minimize the risk of any equipment injuring your genitals. A falling tripod can create an unfortunate chain reaction by entangling other objects, including lights, drapes, plants and other vertically placed decorations. Even in outdoor situations where weather conditions can change at short notice, a falling tripod is almost sure to damage anything attached to it. For both indoor and outdoor photography with medium to large cameras, I suggest using a sand bag with stabilizing weight to hang from the hook located at the bottom of even the simplest tripod's centerpost. With a sandbag attached, you will also minimize the introduction of vibrations.

Chapter 2

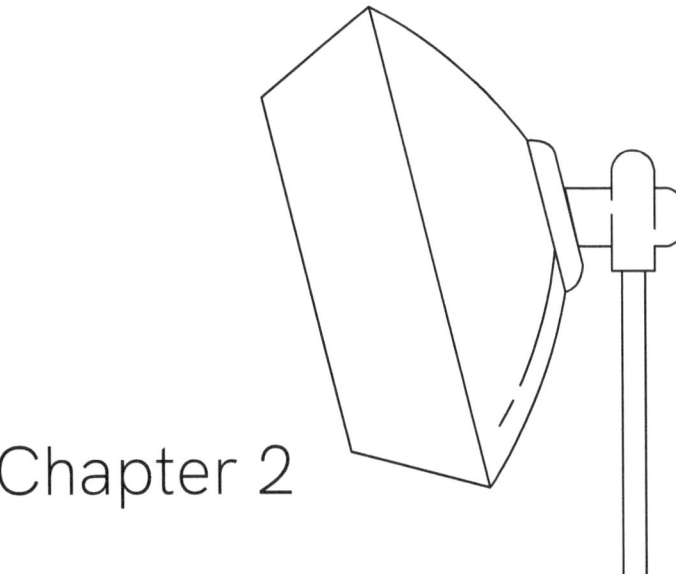

Lighting

While much can be achieved with good equipment and proper grooming, you will soon realize that there are no shortcuts to becoming a truly successful penile photographer. Ultimately, success will depend on a willingness to experiment and your tenacity for fulfilling your creative vision.

Light and Shadows

Learning how to use light and shadows is going to be crucial for your success in penile photography. There are a plethora of available lighting options and there is going to be at least one, possibly many, that will perfectly suit your specific needs to immortalize your penis time and time again. Experimentation, curiosity and a disposition to "break the rules" should be key ingredients in your endeavor. Personally, I am always attempting to achieve a new, ultimate lighting setup and have spent countless hours trying new ideas, testing and evaluating both standardized and unproven alternatives and methods.

Not all, but many photographers are intimidated by the very thought of using a flash or a continuous lighting solution when capturing their penis in best possible light. This despite the fact that just like cameras, which have become simpler to use and more affordable, lighting too has evolved and is now less technically demanding.

There are a wide variety of affordable compact flashes and smartphone-friendly continuous lighting solutions available. I would argue that there are innumerable options for lights and lighting equipment accessories today. And the online tutorials on how to use even the most complex lighting gear are often pedagogical and easy to apply to your penile photography pursuit.

Gone are the hefty, so-called hot lights of yesteryear. Bulbs that invariably get super-hot and make even shorter photo sessions arduous and unbearably uncomfortable. While heat has the physiological advantage of helping to increase the size of a flaccid penis, it can also create unwanted red blush.

Just to be perfectly clear, I'm not stating that old school lighting solutions are to be dismissed or replaced if these are the only available options. Many of these vintage lights can provide exactly what you need. But technology is always evolving and though perhaps not guaranteeing better results, much of today's offerings allow for much more flexibility and take less amount of your time to arrange and rearrange once the shoot has begun. Whenever I devote time to my penile photography hobby, I usually opt for the "less is more" paradigm and let the challenges I must succumb to act as a pilot light to help keep the flame of my creative energy burning.

So-called Speedlites are the most common types of on-camera flashguns but can also be used via a wireless trigger for off-camera shooting. Not all, but some Speedlites offer both a wide range of sync speeds, from multiple bursts at short intervals to really powerful light omitted at lower cycles. Some flashes even offer a continuous lighting option, a modeling light, that can be well-suited for small spaces in need of just a bit more light than what is otherwise available. I find that the modeling light often suffices for more intimate penile photography scenarios.

Many of today's continuous lighting options are lightweight, making them mobile and versatile to setup. Some also offer varying color temperatures, from bright daylight to warm indoor lighting. Today, there are even continuous lights that are soft and foldable. The vast majority are at the very least thin and can run on battery power as well as being connected to a wall socket. Obviously, the fewer cords, cables and wall-connected power cables you have, the less likely you will run into potential tangling situations during a penile photography session.

LED – Light Emitting Diode

Over the past several decades, LED lamps of varying sizes, strengths and color temperatures have steadily replaced more traditional, aforementioned solutions, like tungsten, incandescent and florescent lights. LEDs need considerably less energy while still being a much more efficient light source than filament light when you consider the size and power ratio. For example, a typical LED bulb uses 75% less energy than an incandescent bulb.

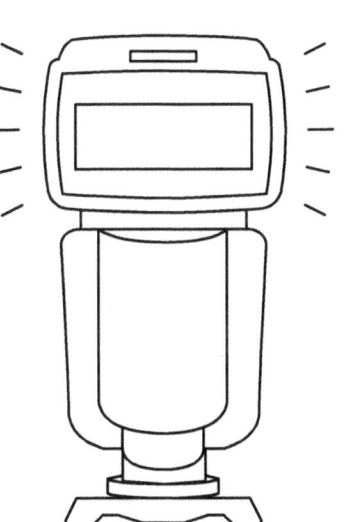

Color temperatures 5000 Kelvin and over are often referred to as "daylight", "cool" or "bluish" colors. Lower color temperatures, between 2700–3000 Kelvin, are often called "warm" or "yellow". For most interior lighting situations, you'll need to take into account that a warmer light (lower color temperature) is often used to accentuate a relaxed environment. A room or business office lit with a higher color temperature can be used to convey more focus and concentration on your penis and genitals.

Warmer temperatures are usually preferable in indoor penile photography settings and the opposite, cooler temperatures, for outdoor sessions. There are, of course, exceptions where, for example, you might want to use a warmer lighting source outdoors. Golden hours, the first hour before sunrise and the last before sunset, are preferably lit with warmer lights to compliment (as opposed to compete) with ambient light.

The largest benefit of using LED lights over heat-generating bulbs, is that you can get really close shots of your penis without risking horrifically painful, slow-healing burns. I've heard anecdotally, about situations where pubic hair catches fire and scars the soft and sensitive underlying flesh of a penis.

Equally important to consider with light is indisputably how shadows help shape and frame your penile photography efforts. I enjoy using the shadows created by the penis and testicles as an intentional part of the composition. Shadows can become an important part of a photograph. The art here is not allowing a shadow to unintentionally dominate or "take over" the scene you are trying to create. Personally, I find silhouette photography interesting. Capturing just the outline of an erect or semi-flaccid penis can certainly achieve a goal of conveying its shape, length and girth.

Using only a single light source means you must use shadows creatively to your benefit by placing the light source where it does the most for your artistic vision. If you don't have a professional grade lens at your disposal and experience reoccurring difficulties when trying to create some kind of visible depth between your penis in the foreground and a background, I suggest rethinking your entire setup. Maybe you need to start taking your penile photography more seriously!

So-called "high-key lighting" is an excellent option for confident photographers who wish to showcase their penis in the most perfect light. Here, I typically use two individual light sources pointing from just behind the waist and directly at the penis and one light source positioned from the front, usually somewhere below or above the camera. This setup will eliminate, or, at least seriously reduce any hard, contrasty shadows. It goes without saying that this style of photography takes some planning and necessary equipment.

Daylight coming from a window should not be dismissed. Soft, almost shadowless winter light, can work wonders as an ambient light source. Without much effort, I find that curtains and drapes

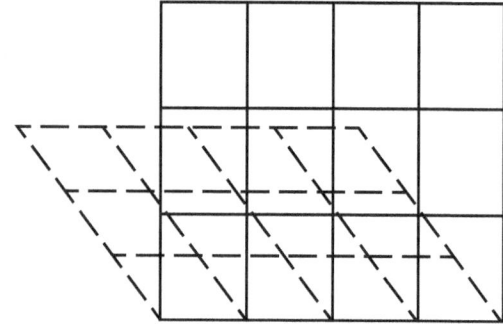

can also help modify or adjust the window light. Arranging a photo session so that you have the option to take full advantage of outdoor light while indoors is highly recommended. I find that though seldom my only light source, outdoor light can be useful as a "filler" that helps reduce unwarranted contrast from an artificial light source.

Be aware, however, that mixed lighting conditions (daylight and indoor) can potentially create so-called color casts and unwanted, unattractive skin hues on, or, around the penis – which might offset more attractive attributes and qualities in your final composition. We will cover more on post processing in a later chapter.

Natural light is almost always good when photographing your penis. This partially explains why many penile photographers choose outdoor locations, albeit that this choice doesn't come without risks when compared with photographing at home, in the office or other indoor locations which are safer and easier to control from unwanted onlookers.

Outdoor penile photography can be very rewarding, too! However, you should proceed with caution. In many countries, public nudity in general is strictly illegal. If caught and prosecuted, you might be looking at being sentenced to a multiyear incarceration and forced to pay very steep fines. In Australia, indecent exposure refers specifically to the genital areas, while in Germany full nudity is mandatory in certain naturalist areas.

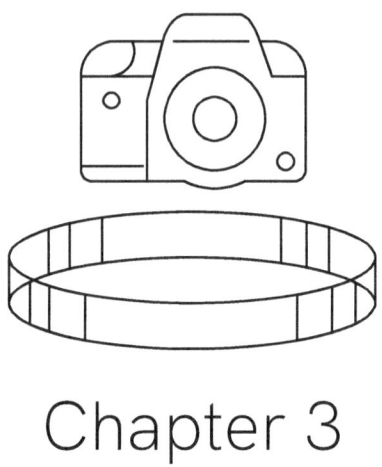

Chapter 3

Angles, Focal Regions and Targeted Adjustments

As the ancient idiom goes, beauty is in the eye of the beholder. But often times a beholder is unknowledgeable and lost in an infinite labyrinth of aesthetic confusion. They are in desperate need of qualified guidance. Therefore, it is up to you, dear fellow penile photographer, to counsel, (not sure you should use the word coerce) coerce and connect them to the best possible image you can create of your penis. This process will take time. But once achieved, and you will eventually reach this pivotal moment, viewers will feel so immeasurably pleased and emotional absorbed, they will inevitably desire more and more images of your penis. This must be your mantra going forward. (A bit creepy sounding)

Setting aside technical aspects for a moment, in penile photography, there are no "right" angles. Defining what is beautiful and what is ugly is largely subject to individual tastes and preferences. The most important objective for a penile photographer is the ability to communicate or connect with the viewer. The subject matter, the penis, should be able to convey the intended "story" through the photographer's choice of angle, composition, lighting and a series of targeted adjustments.

I believe that photographing your own penis in an aesthetically pleasing and intriguing way is possibly the most difficult of all self-portraiture genres. Discovering, mostly through experimentation, the best angle and focal region is a time-consuming and sometimes frustrating task. You can certainly get lucky and capture a wonderful photograph of your penis within only a few minutes. But repeating this over time will prove that there are no shortcuts to professional level penile photography.

At the very onset of this pursuit, I suggest using a mirror. I've found that a square mirror that essentially has more or less the same dimensions as the camera's sensor or, alternatively, the width and length of the final printed photograph you have in mind, will be the most useful. Use the mirror to test angles by placing it at or near the same location as you will be shooting from. For the handyman, attaching a mirror to a selfie-stick can prove to provide a very efficient way of experimenting with the different angles you have available. Like the Polaroid camera was used as a faster, less expensive way to get a preview of a lighting setup and photographic composition throughout much of the 1970s, 1980s and 1990s, before the era of digital photography, a selfie-stick can be used to experiment with different angles.

Achieving the best possible angle of your penis is going to take some time. Be patient. Firstly, you must determine at what stage you prefer the penis to be at before embarking on the session. You can, of course, have the objective to shoot a series of images with the ambition to capture various stages and phases in which the penis's length and girth evolve.

The Soft and Flaccid Penis

Only when the brain, nerves and blood vessels, together with hormones, work in conjunction, causing the spongy chambers (corpora cavernosa and corpus spongiosum) to swell, can the penis begin to become erect.

The Swollen and Tumescent Penis

To achieve visible arousal, a male needs to use either his senses, sight or touch, or thoughts, recollections or pure fantasies. Stimulating his nerves, physically or mentally, will inevitably cause blood vessels in the penis and its aforementioned spongy chambers to expand. With more blood flowing in than out, the penis will begin to inflate and stretch way beyond its resting size.

Full erection

If arousal continues, the nerves between the man's penis and brain keep moving more blood into the penis which is simultaneously kept from flowing back out. Ultimately, the penis becomes hard and rigid, and a so-called "boner" is achieved.

Variety of Rigidity

Every penis is unique. In how quickly it transitions from limp to fully erect, in the hardness of the erection and the shape it takes once fully engorged. A penis can be a 'shower' – large in flaccid state, but does not increase much as it gets erect. Or it can be a 'grower' – small as flaccid but grows impressively when erect. And an erect penis may decide to deflate at the most inopportune times. I am sure you will agree about how fascinating, yet seemingly uncontrollable, this process actually is.

Patience is necessary when photographing your penis. A stoic attitude also helps. In all honesty, I have experienced many situations where I was unable to achieve a level of erectness that I wanted and needed for a particular penile photography session. That said, I can actually make good use of circumstances when I am unable to go beyond semi-erect. At this stage, I find the penis to be quite malleable, allowing me to bend it and create interesting angles and perspectives. With perhaps a few biological deviations, for most men, it is impossible to maintain a certain level of erectness for more than a few precious moments. And it is here where a high level of preparedness in order to take advantage of a guaranteed fleeting

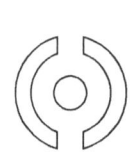

moment is crucial – especially if you have a particular stage or phase of the penis's swelling that you aim to capture and perpetuate.

Focal Regions

While experimenting with different angles before principle penis photography begins is unquestionably important, deciding on focal region beforehand is nothing less than paramount. Here I feel compelled to help you understand the penis's various physical parts, or, the penis anatomy. This is so you will feel more familiar with penile photography terms like "Dorsal View" and "Ventral View", once you begin deciding on focal regions and depth of field.

Photographing the Penis; Basic Anatomy

The penis consists of the base where the penis begins to extend beyond the body itself, the shaft or trunk (if you prefer using a tree as a metaphor), the glans or cap (not entirely dissimilar in shape to a hat, helmet or in some extreme cases, a Portobello or Shiitake mushroom), and the foreskin. Circumcised men have little or no foreskin.

Internally, but often visible on the outside and along the shaft and glans of the penis, is the dorsal nerve, several blood vessels and, of course the urethra opening from which both urine, prostate secretion and semen are voluntarily or involuntarily discharged.

As I am sure you are well aware, the anatomy of the penis comes in many variants of shapes, sizes and circumferences. Probably as many forms as there are men. No two men have analogous penises, not even identical twin males. I believe that each of the penis's parts can be photographed to an aesthetically pleasing level. Obviously, it is the various parts of the penis that make up the whole organ. But I have nonetheless experienced many, many sessions where I chose a particular angle and focal region that did not necessarily reveal the entirety of my penis. For example, focusing on a clearly visible vein or blood vessel and the texture surrounding it can provide for very interesting and creatively inspiring compositions. In fact, in my bedroom, I have a large print of a blood vessel just below the head or glans shot with a macro lens taken from the penis's ventral view. Unsuspecting viewers of this print do not know that the visually pleasing abstract photograph is actually my penis.

My advice is to let go of preconceptions and obvious choices and instead attempt to break new ground within penile photography. To each is own, as the saying goes. Depending on what my objective is, I always aim to first and foremost create images that please me and provide a level of satisfaction that justifies the time and effort invested in a session. Sure, there will be failures and seemingly insurmountable challenges along the way. Penile photography is possibly the hardest genre of them all. Which, on the other hand, also makes it the most interesting.

*Within philosophy, aesthetics is the study of beauty and taste as related to the study of sensory values. In visual arts, aesthetics refers to the attractiveness of a particular animate or inanimate subject matter.

*A selfie stick is used by photographers and videographers to position a smartphone or action camera beyond the reach of an arm. With a selfie stick, the photographer or videographer is able to capture images at unique angles and distances normally unattainable when only using a human arm.

Selfie sticks are usually telescopic, designed so that the user can determine the length or reach of the still camera or video recorder depending on location and situation At the shaft of a standard selfie stick is a handle. This is where the extendable parts of the stick are housed and also, at least when fully retracted, where some kind of clamp mechanism is located. There are many selfie sticks available today that can easily be connected to an action camera or smartphone through either a wired connector or wirelessly (tethered) via short distance radio technology known more popularly as Bluetooth.

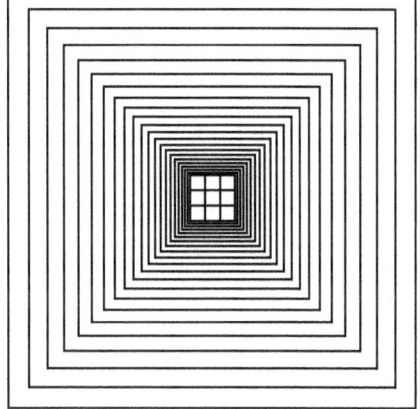

Chapter 4

Penis Photography and Psychology

Psychology is an important aspect of most human endeavors, and certainly so for photography. Given the intimate nature of penile photography, it includes a deeply personal psychology of you – the photographer – and the perceptual psychology of the viewer. While some photographers claim that the camera is a mirror of the mind and soul, I do not feel quite so strongly about this. I experiment a lot and quite often the results look so different from anything that could be considered my mind or my soul. However my own personal psychology becomes more apparent in the image selection phases when I choose what to share with others, what to archive and which images to discard.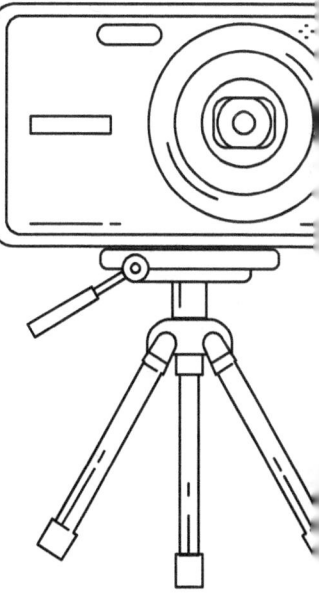

Reality is shaped by the photographer and interpreted by the viewer. Photography, even the most realistic and editorialized is therefore never really a 100% accurate representation. It is a representation of what we wish to save or preserve. Photography is a way to freeze time, to visually capture one's own experience, our personal perspective with a tangible and preserved form. With choices in lighting, shape and composition, the pe-

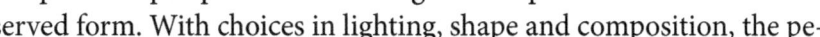

nile photographer interprets a snapshot of his experience or the experience he wishes to communicate. An experienced penile photographer will help viewers focus on esthetics that would perhaps otherwise be ignored. A well lighted penis can convey a large range of emotions. Our lives and our bodies are always changing, with increasing age we grow in confidence and self-acceptance while our physical body decays. The penile photographer does not take these phases of life for granted and undertands the value of documenting those moments in our lives that would otherwise be forgotten and lost in time.

The more you understand the psychology involved with photographing your penis, the better these photos will ultimately become. It helps to understand that it is you, the photographer, that must help the viewer use their interpretational skills. Your empathetic ability to relate to others and your understanding of their interpretation process will allow you to capture your penis in ways that stimulate interest and appreciation. A well-composed penis photograph can, if done mindfully, reflect the soul and thoughts you wish to convey.

A sloppy mindlessly taken photograph of your penis only conveys that you are not interested in the viewer's experience. It communicates a self-centered, narcissistic approach, as if your penis deserves respect regardless of the effort taken to visually capture it. A beautiful penis photo with creative fragmentary and evocative elements can evoke feelings of warmth, love, joy, anticipation, pride, strength and vulnerability. For every photograph it is always the photographer's technical ability and psyche that creates the uniqueness and emotional content communicated through an image.

The interpretation of visual stimuli is the focus of perceptual psychology, and this area of psychology offers us some interesting concepts to consider and experiment with.

Similarity

This simple concept involves the recognition of patterns. These patterns can be in colors, in lines or other visual elements. The brain automatically creates visual patterns to comprehend the environment. I like to use the concept of similarity to create a sense of unity or harmony within a penile photograph. For example, using accessories that either resemble the penis, certain elements of the penis or round, oval shaped objects that generate a perception of similarity with the testicles. This is a good principle for beginners to start experimenting as impressive results are relatively easy to attain.

Continuity

Continuity refers to the principle of lines and directionality. Our brains, just like our minds, tend to follow lines in one direction. This is enhanced when the lines lead us somewhere logical. Continuity is a very versatile principle for penile photography as it allows the penis to be photographed in various environments and against different backgrounds yet remain the focus of attention thanks to the use of the continuity principle. When creating an aesthetic with this principle, I like to lead the viewer on a subtle continuous path towards the penis, or the sub-element I wish to enhance.

Our brain instinctively dislikes missing information and therefore it fills in the gaps. This is called "closure". As an example, consider words with the letters rearranged such as "my pnise si baeluitfu" (my penis is beautiful). The words are comprehensible despite being jumbled as the brain automatically helps us rearrange the information to make it understandable. While not the same process, this is similar to how the brain fills in fragmented photographic images. If there is missing information, or negative space, our brains will try to fill in the information to make sense of the image. When, for example, the background you choose for a penile photograph is similar in color, hue and lighting to the organ itself, the brain works hard to find lines that help to identify and, ultimately, distinguish elements within the image.

Figure and Ground

The basis for this principle is that our brain uses light and shadows to differentiate a figure from a foreground and background. With your choice of lighting, you can make your penis blend in with the background or visually pop out from it. By

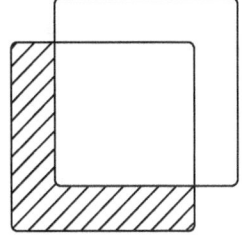

using similar color tones your penis will seem blended with the background whereas by using color contrasts your penis will "jump out" of the photo. I enjoy experimenting with subtle application of this principle by allowing the penis to discreetly contrast with the backgrounds. Or, for an opposite effect, a larger penis will seem less obtrusive when slightly blended with the background. The simplest way to make your penis or one or both testicles pop is by opening up the aperture, thereby letting more light in – somewhere between f/1.4 and 2.8 usually works for me.

Chapter 5

Self Timer and Remote Release Exposure Devices'

Lighting conditions, camera, and artistic vision will determine if a self-timer or remote release device is the most applicable way to capture penile imagery. Both have intrinsic technical advantages and downsides and I will attempt to cover as much of these as I can in this chapter.

Going Old School: Using a Self-Timer

Though one might assume that just because a self-timer functionality on a camera is self explanatory and therefore uncomplicated to make use of, there are still several issues that need to be carefully adressed. In photography terms, the self-timer function on a camera or smartphone is a relatively new technology that has yet to fully replace a wired or even a wireless, remote exposure release device. Personally, I find that using a self-timer to trigger when I want a camera to capture a photo of my penis to be somewhat stressful. Although you likely won't

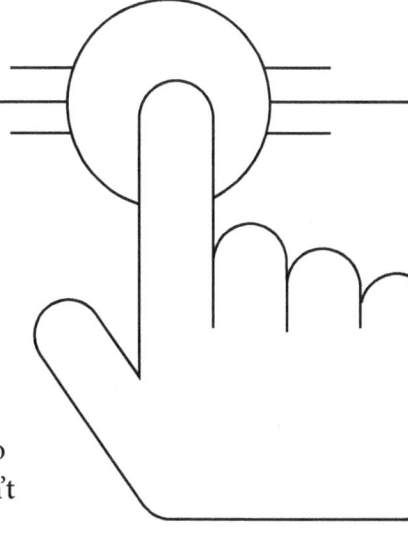

have to worry about a release cable (when using a wired remote release device) getting in your way, there is always a risk of it unintentionally becoming an unwanted object in your composition. Even if you are proficient in post-processing applications like Adobe Photoshop, Pixelmator or GIMP and can retouch and remove undesired objects relatively easy, this will of course take additional time to remedy. Time that could have been spent on more important, worthy objectives.

While the default settings of a typical smartphone's builtin self-timer function might have limitation in regard to how long of a delay between triggering the exposure button and the camera actually taking the photograph, there are many third-party applications for both the iOS and Android platforms that provide considerably more options. Many of these "apps" are free and some have upgrades you must pay (in-app purchases) for but that then unlock additional features and settings, providing you with even more possibilities.

For me, the problem with using a self-timer is the obvious concern about having the ability to trigger the exposure and still having enough time to resume my position. Penile photography is full of variables that include allowing adequate time for the penis to reach the intended level of erectness and hopefully being able to maintain this fleeting state long enough for the composition to be captured according to my vision.

There are smartphone applications and even some dedicated cameras (point and shoot, DSLR and mirrorless) that allow you to decide on the length of the delayed exposure, i.e. when the shutter exposes the sensor and the photograph, or a series of photographs are taken, many have just two settings, short and longer. The shorter time setting is naturally far too short for it to be useful in this context and I find that even the extended delay alternative does not provide sufficient time for me to reestablish myself in front of the camera. Practice makes perfect, and I am sure that if only I had the patience, the longer window of the extended delay might actually be able to

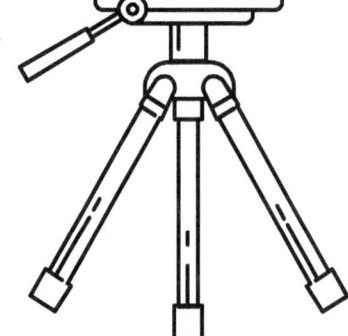

work for me. However, I am more committed to taking several images, a large series even, during each of my devoted penile photography sessions. Running back and forth between the remote exposure trigger and the position I wish my penis to be photographed at, would, to say the least, be tremendously stressful and without doubt have a considerable negative impact on my creative vision.

Capturing your penis wirelessly

While some selfie sticks allow you to trigger your smartphone camera's shutter button wirelessly via Bluetooth or Wifi, there are third party applications or programs that enable you to use another smartphone to do this. Using one smartphone and a specific application, you can in other words trigger the camera's shutter button you are using for penile photography. This is definitely useful, especially when you use the delayed shutter release functionality. Today, modern smartphones can download and make use of a dedicated application to remotely control most of the major camera brands camera functionalities.

If, for example, you used a 10 or 15 second delay setting, this will then give you ample time to hide the smartphone used to remotely trigger the main camera, so that it doesn't become a disturbing object or unwanted prop in your final penile photographs.

I have had very positive and creatively liberating experiences using my smartphone during penile photography. In some cases, the functionality and settings options are identical to what is available when standing behind the camera itself. When settings like aperture, exposure, ISO and even focus can be manipulated and locked remotely, there really is no need to look any further. At least to the extent that you have made all the other variable adjustments including height, angle, lighting and focal length beforehand.

There are high end, professional studio tripods that allow remote adjustment of height and angle and even advanced systems that can let you remotely adjust the focal length of a zoom lens. And while this might be an option for those readers that have more or less unlimited budgets, the vast majority of penile photographers with normal financial constraints, will find that these solutions come at way too steep a price. I assume that like myself, most would prefer to make smaller, more manageable investments which add affordable value.

Using a remote release, regardless of whether or not it is wired or wireless, will take some time to learn and adjust to. This is distinctly true when it comes to using camera software on a smartphone to remotely control a camera. Wireless connectivity has most definitely improved during the last three to five years and is today both stable and reliable. Still, connecting two completely different electronic devices, produced by entirely separate yet purportedly cooperating companies, which is often the case with a manufacturer of DSLR cameras and a smartphone brand, can cause a wide range of at times frustrating technical hurdles. Such hurdles must be overcome with tenacity as different versions of Bluetooth, firmware and other potential software incompatibilities, getting your smartphone to "speak" with your camera can take some time. I find that when this happens, mostly without warning or logical explanation, turning off each of the involved devices, including the smartphone, camera, wifi router and any other networking equipment you may have, and then restarting each of (in no particularly favorable order), will often allow for a solid, lasting connection.

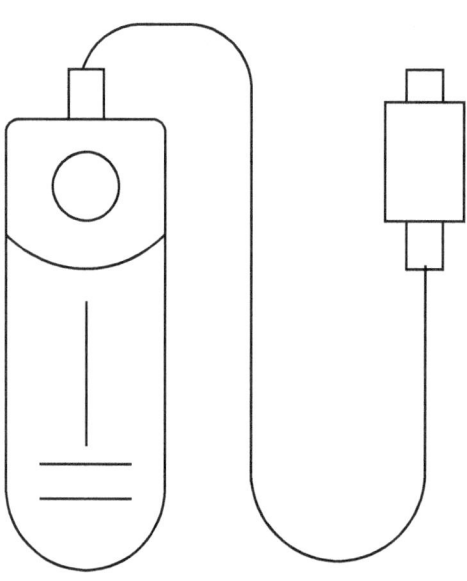

I cannot emphasize enough how important it is here to make sure that the batteries on each of the involved devices are fully charged. I would have saved myself many moments of irritation and frustration had I only checked the battery status of the devices I was using and counting on to work with during my first few penile photography sessions. Having to wait for a smartphone battery to be fully charged, a process that can take up to an hour, can diminish the creative inspiration of even the most patient penile photographer.

Wired Shutter Release Triggering

Even if I do prefer using a wireless shutter release triggering mechanism these days, preferably through a smartphone interface, I have had considerable positive experiences with a traditional wired shutter release via a cable.

Far from all of today's cameras support the oldest type of screw-in release mechanism. On those that do support this somewhat archaic yet still useful feature, there will be a threaded cavity inside the camera's shutter release button where you can screw in the head of the wired release. More common among modern cameras are shutter release connectivity via a so-called port, usually visible after opening a small hinged door located on either side of the camera body. Depending entirely on the model and how advanced it is, on one end of the remote shutter release cable you will either find a simple button mechanism or a thicker, larger control panel which might even be featured with a small screen.

The remote shutter release solution is often equipped with several different functions, one of the most popular being used during time lapse photography. For those unfamiliar with time lapse photography, this involves taking a collection of images captured at a predetermined interval and subsequently compositing these photos in sequence, either straight from the camera or after some post processing, and afterwards creating a video that shows a series of movements compressed over time. Though interesting and not without its creative and technical challenges, I have yet to find time lapse useful or even suitable within my own penile photography.

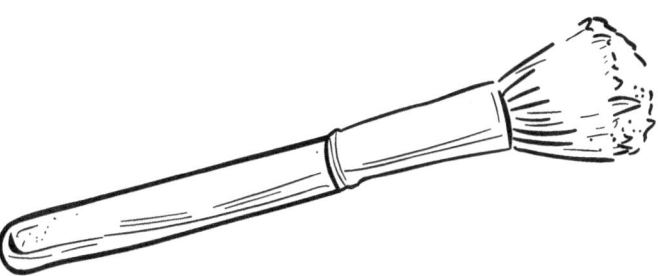

Chapter 6

Makeup or Natural

One might think that choosing whether or not to use the help of cosmetics to manipulate color tones, cover uneven and unwanted textures, hide temporary blemishes, would be a simple decision. In my experience, nothing could be further from the truth. This chapter will attempt to weigh the pros and cons and cover a few thoughtful suggestions and ideas.

Much of what can be done with makeup prior to a penile photography session, can theoretically, also be achieved in the post processing phase. Software applications like Adobe Photoshop and Procreate offer a wealth of virtual tools and countless options to alter color, tint, temperature, sharpness, focal point and much else in a photograph. While changing format and size, reversing perspectives and cropping the final composition are accomplished relatively straight-forwardly and therefore easy to do, performing retouching, cloning skin and reshaping (including enlarging and reducing) takes a fundamental understanding of how these tools work and which methods are the most proven to use to accomplish your goal.

When using Adobe Photoshop, I always take advantage of the layer features and make sure I am working on a digital copy and never perform any adjustments or alterations on the underlying, original reference composition. Once all of my genital photos are safely transferred to my computer, I make a copy of all of the session's images and subsequently only work on the duplicate versions. That way, I always have the originals to bounce back to, should I need to do so.

Even if you are not already familiar with the aforementioned software editing programs, to the extent that you perhaps know what they can help you achieve but are unfamiliar with how to use them to reach your vision, there are a plethora of both richly illustrated text based and video based tutorials online – most of which are made available for free (albeit often supported through advertising).

Makeup and Cosmetics

You can either choose to invest in a tidy collection of makeup items and spend time practicing how to aptly apply various shades of powder, cream and balm on your penis and scrotum in order to achieve a specific look and maybe cover up unwanted details. Or, you could spend approximately an equal amount of time educating yourself with dedicated computer software and soon learn how to realize similar results during the post-production process.

Of course you can also do both. In fact, I encourage this. By learning both what can be achieved in post production and the characteristics of various types of make up, you will come to appreciate the advantages and limitations of each approach and possibly, how to combine the two.

Here I would like to emphasize that when you do buy cosmetic products, that you choose those which have been tested for allergies and hypersensitive skin types. Furthermore, I personally prefer supporting cosmetic companies that sell products which have not been tested on animals of any kind.

As this is where much of the body's erogenous zone is found, the skin on the penis, scrotum and surrounding area is distinctly soft, thin and densely quilted with nerves. As most penile photographers are likely aware, this region is not only sensitive to temperature fluctuations, it also responds remarkably fast to physical pressure and, of course, even the lightest touch. A warm lamp or cold breeze coming from an open window can also create wanted or unfavorable results.

I mention this in a precautionary context when preparing for a penile photography session with the intention of applying cream, lotion, balm or any other kind of cosmetics on or around the genital area prior to photographing. I have often found that the makeup application process itself will likely create a slight, involuntary reaction, sometimes with a degree of tingling delight, that will unavoidably render an unintended visual alteration in girth and length of the penis and to a lesser degree, the scrotum. This occurs repeatedly even when I've added small amounts of makeup as lightly, slowly and surreptitiously as possible.

All told, today, I tend to choose not to utilize any makeup or cosmetics during penile photography sessions. The disadvantages are easily outweighed by the disadvantages. I find it just takes too much time to accurately apply cosmetics – particularly considering the above mentioned risk of physical reaction and a potential shift in the entire composition. In sessions where pubic hair will invariably be visible, I also find it very difficult to avoid adding lotions and creams in unwanted areas or parts of the penis I feel are best left bare and without manipulation. Perhaps it's just me and that you will instead experience that applying makeup is in fact time-saving, enjoyable and considerably easier than what I described above.

Nature offers Natural Beauty

After many years of penile photography, and perhaps in part due to my heritage and cultural breeding with a reverence for minimalism, I believe that less is more. I realize this is a reoccurring theme in this book. Yet I still feel compelled to reiterate that my extensive experience and research has consistently guided me towards this approach. There have certainly been times and occasions in past and recent years where I deviated from this path. I am only human, and can be lured to stray from what I know is the only way forward.

I have tried many different types of makeup, props, advanced pubic hair styling and occasionally, even seriously pondered having cosmetic surgery performed to better achieve an artistic vision. Fortunately, these outlandish thoughts were fleeting and after realizing that what I was actually aspiring for was to replace my current lack of creative originality and photographic inventiveness with a unique, albeit surgically altered look. Such creative doldrums are commonplace in all kinds of creative endeavors, and we don't always recognize them for what they truly are. I have often felt downtrodden by doubts and insecurity and allowed myself to get distracted by superficial, often quick solutions, instead of looking at the real issue at hand. Penile photography is not commercial photography and only in an erotic or pornographic context can it be considered an editorial genre. I have always seen penile photography as an art form in its own right. A way to visualize and express the celebration of the penis and, to a lesser degree, the scrotum.

Accepting and Respecting the Penis

Considerably more important then refining a composition, choosing which camera and lighting setup to use, is embracing acceptance. Serious penile photography demands that you come to terms with and feel perfectly comfortable looking, touching, shaping and, yes, even admiring your penis and all of its attributes.

Initially, I found this quite difficult to comply with. Like many men, I was never entirely satisfied with the way my penis looked. Its slightly bent shape and the way the left testicle seems to have almost twice the circumference as the right was disturbing to me throughout most of my teen years. I had an unrealistic view of how my genitals should have been perfectly symmetric, which was likely fueled by an overshadowing narrative from schoolbooks where beautifully illustrated penises inadvertently disallowed physiological divergencies.

Thankfully, as soon as I entered high school, I understood how diverse the penis and scrotum could be – that no two penises were identical.

There were just too many variables for two men to have the exact same shapes, lengths, girths and pubic hair type.

In my late 20s, I discovered how taking photographs of my penis could be incredibly therapeutic, cathartic even, in regards to accepting and fully appreciating the way things are. The many, many hours of in-depth penile photography sessions have no doubt had a tremendous influence on my relationship with my penis and I feel convinced that it has been instrumental at improving my capacity to engage and ultimately find pleasure in my own desires. Today, I clearly feel an increased level of confidence in my relationship with my penis, much thanks to penile photography.

As far as the human anatomy is concerned, I find the penis to be the by far most interesting body part. Its seamless, shape-shifting ability has always fascinated me. Although a woman's complex genitalia and reproductive system is certainly engaging, the penis is naturally more exposed, extrovert and its soft, aerodynamic contours offer endless photographical variation.

Dear reader, I am here to tell you that once you've come to terms with the natural shape and physiological composition as well as the functionality of your penis and scrotum, penile photography will become more joyous and you will be able to pursue a slew of perhaps previously untried and unappreciated angles and perspectives without judgment, and without fickleness.

Even if I personally prefer a naturalistic approach to penile photograph, one without makeup and manscaping or even props, I am somewhat beholden to the seemingly infinite retouching and targeted adjustment possibilities once the image is transfered to my computer. With my minimalistic mindset still intact, I have absolutely no ethical qualms about cautiously and respectfully modifying my penile imagery so that it connects with the creative vision that initially possessed me.

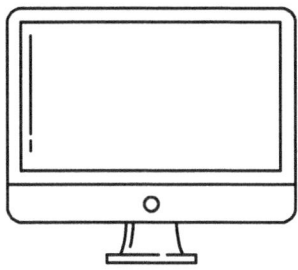

Chapter 7

Composition in the Post Processing and Editing Phase of Penile Imagery

In penile photography like in many other digital visual artforms, much can be accomplished in post-processing as long as the digital image in question contains a reasonable amount of image information. Which is why I strongly suggest using a dedicated camera or smartphone that produces images that which allow you to make relevant adjustments and plenty of creative options after the fact.

Viewing a Composition

Penile photography is not fully appreciated by every-one. Sometimes your creative efforts will not even be noticed by the viewer. This is essentially true within all forms and expressions of art. I find that a photograph needs to exist in my mind for a while in order for it to have sufficient time and opportunity to be absorbed and become something I better understand and respect over time.

I mention this because it should be something to consider and prepare yourself for before finalizing the penile images you intend to archive, publish, distribute, exhibit or sell.

In my experience where and when I have spoken to fellow penile photographers, I often find that many actually confuse the definition of penile photography. Generally, people seem to look upon it merely as either a subgenre of mainstream pornography or as living within the questionably objective realm of documentary photography.

However, my opinion on how to designate and categorize serious penile photography – as opposed to the often hastily, thoughtlessly captured snapshots intended for dubious dating sites, similar platforms and distribution venues – is to look upon it as an artform in its own right. I am not dismissing every other bodily part as unworthy of photographic attention, nor am I trying to negate the well-documented overabundance of subject matters, topics, genres or even the more or less obscure sub-categories that exist within erotic photography. Not at all! It's just that when you think about it on a metaphysical plane, what could possibly be more interesting to portray photographically than the penis, a living organ that enables our very existence on this planet?

Composition Rules and Roles

Filling the Frame

Busy backgrounds and surroundings can, and likely will, distract from the main point of focus. By cropping tightly in the post processing phase, you will simultaneously be eliminating the risk of the background receiving so much attention that it figuratively overshadows your main subject. This is particularly important in penile photography where you are attempting to capture something as intimate as the penis and scrotum. If the session is taking place outdoors, say, in a busy location where the background is most certainly going to be moving and inherently generating a distraction, or, where texture and patterns behind the penis can possibly confuse viewers ability to follow your intended vi-

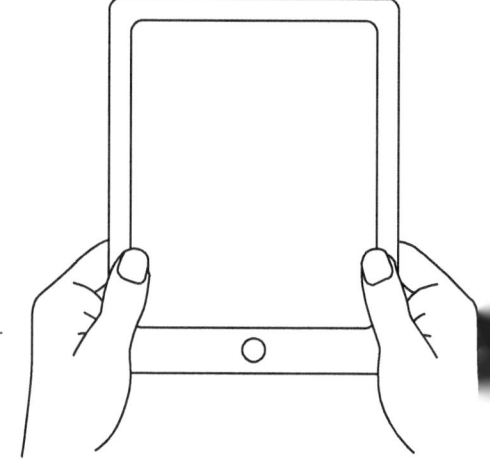

sual lead, cropping tightly is highly recommended.

Finally, professional penile photographers and enthusiastic amateurs alike will often take advantage and make use of various surrounding objects, natural or manmade, to frame the penis and thereby add scale and draw the viewers eye towards a specific, preferential part of the penile image. A plant, an array of cacti, a small sculpture or perhaps a bar of colorful soap might be just what you need to emphasize or deemphasize scale, size, depth of field and focus.

Rule of thirds

The rule of thirds is the most basic rule or guideline to follow within photography and visual arts. In essence, the objective of the rule of thirds is to create a more interesting composition. By adding nine equally spaced vertical and horizontal lines in a frame, you will create sections into which you can place your subject matter. You frame your subject matter on either a vertical or horizontal line where they meet at one third of the upper or lower pattern. This technique works particularly well for landscape penile photography and I have seen many outstanding examples of penile images where the penis and scrotum together are used inventively as part of a intimate landscape composition.

Breaking the Rules While Striking a Balance

Though I definitely think bending and even breaking the rules can benefit your penile photography (and all other art forms you may be involved with) and should always be something to consider when abiding by them, this approach should not be a means to an end. In other words, breaking or bending the rules always needs to deliver a new take and something so unconventional that it perhaps even creates a new set of aesthetic rules and ultimately pushes the envelope, opens doors, promotes disruption and offers many new possibilities.

Applications like Procreate and Photoshop will provide you with an almost endless amount of tools to adjust, adapt, amend and change what your camera captured. If you already are proficient with these software applications and are sufficiently computer savvy in general, or, once you have familiarized yourself with what can potentially be accomplished, temptation may just become too overwhelming to resist. At its core, I see the computer as an extensions to my penile imagery. While the penis itself is captured using a series of manual or automatic settings (exposure, aperture, light sensitivity and so forth) on the camera's sensor, I have always seen this as just the beginning of the creative process.

The amount of information, in number of pixels, their size and quality have been stored in the image file of your photograph, will determine how much maneuverable scope you will have on your digital palette. A "medium" sized penile photograph at 7 megapixels, will not be as malleable as one of 25 megapixels. Even if all digital editing applications allow you to interpolate or, add interpretations (pixels) of synthesized image information, the quality of these renditions can often be quite revealing and difficult to manipulate with good end results. In my experience, interpolations offer the best possible results when enlarging the final penile image before it is to be printed. If the end use is on-screen viewing only, there really is no reason or benefit of interpolating an image.

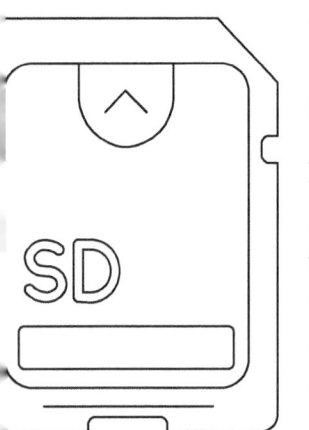

If you have used a smartphone with a low megapixel count for your penile photography session, the results from manipulating an upscaled image (through interpolation) will likely not be satisfactory at all. However, with more and higher quality pixels, you will certainly find that there is enough image information to allow you to both crop in on the penis or scrotum, alter or adjust color temperature, retouch blemishes and other imperfections that you feel distract attention.

I believe I have been very clear about my choice of preferring to manipulate skin tones and making minor color adjustments in a computer using a software program like Adobe Photoshop over applying makeup before the session begins. And through a copious quantity of failures and retakes over the years, I have self-educated myself on how to best produce results similar to what a professional makeup artist is capable of delivering. This choice, at the basic level, provides me with the widest amount of options insofar that if I end up not fully appreciating the results from the physical make-up I had applied before a penile photography session, it will be quite difficult to remove in the post processing phase. Conversely, if I photograph a penis without any makeup with a reasonably high quantity camera and neutral but thoughtful lighting, I will have much more leeway to add vibrance, saturation, contrast and sharpening during the post processing phase.

I encourage you to use all available tools and methods with honesty and authenticity.

I'll end this chapter by sharing my workflow during post processing.

Insert memory card or connect smartphone and import images to a dedicated folder on the computer or tablet

Open all images in editing software application (Lightroom or Photoshop)

Adjust image exposure

Set color temperatures (warm, cold or neutral)

Increase focus (gently)

Crop final image

Save and archive (or, print)

Before the age of personal computers capable of editing high resolution photographs, just before the dawn of Apple's Macintosh and and portable PCs, I developed all of my 35mm negatives and positive slides in a traditional "dark room". By using an enlarger, noxious fluids in developing trays, as well as tongs, tweezers, gloves, and squeegees, I (was or wasn't?) was able to realize many of my creative ideas.

Chapter 8

Publishing and Distribution thoughts (copyright protection + Ethics and post-#metoo.

Never in the history of the arts has the public discourse been so preoccupied with equality and political correctness as in this current day and age. Visualizing images of nudity publicly, either online, in a gallery setting or otherwise, can and will likely cause great contention and, at times, even outrage. Ironically, thanks to the Internet, there has never before been more freely available access to sexually explicit content, including traditional erotica, various varieties of pornography and a wide range of what some consider to be both bizarre and perverse.

It is within this most delicate epoch that penile art and other serious art forms susceptible to sensitive, easily angered and often overly prejudice viewership strive to exist and flourish.

Mindful Penile Photography

Understanding that not everyone can cast away inherited or learned bias and prejudgments will serve you well as a serious penile photographer. I completely appreciate your enthusiasm for this wonderful photographic genre and all that it can provide you with creatively. I also understand that the joy can at times seem boundless. To this day, I often feel an almost irresistible, uncontrollable urge to share my art work with the world. But since distribution via the Internet, text messaging applications, web based and dedicated email clients are readily available to all, it is ultimately your responsibility to do what you can to keep your images from being indiscriminately exposed to sensitive viewers and inappropriate audiences.

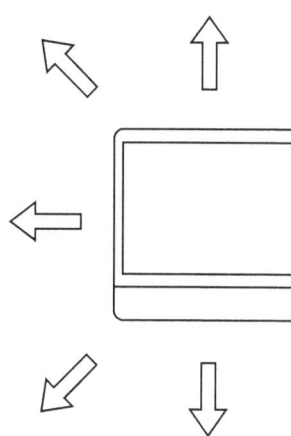

In addition to considering ethical, religious and cultural implications, I strongly suggest that you also ensure that all of your penile images are distributed within the judicial boundaries of your location. Knowing that your creative art work will be viewed and appreciated, if not exclusively, then at the very least to an intended majority viewership, by an audience both pre-pared for and equipped to enjoy, embrace and be immersed by penile photography, will likely give you significant peace of mind.

Why being critical is always beneficial

Unless you are temporarily collaborating, which some prefer to do as a means and method to increase knowledge and expand creatively, penile photography is a lonely venture. The entire process; deciding location, choosing a suitable background, selecting camera and appropriately accompanying lens, as well as designing a lighting setup, is a certainly a solitary process. And then comes the post processing phase, which can absorb numerous lonely hours. Finally it is time to decide what you wish to do with the penile images and how and where you might share or exhibit these unique photographs.

Being your own editor, reviewer and critic is an inevitable part of being an artist, regardless of level and medium. Making selections, choosing which images to keep – and perhaps edit – and which to throw away and delete forever, is without any hesitation the toughest and most frustrating aspect of the creative procedure within penile photography.

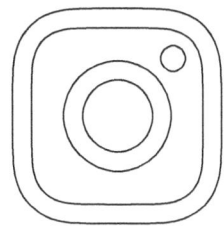

Each penile photo session is unique, and depending on if editing commences directly afterwards or is purposely or unintentionally delayed, your frame of mind, between capture and post processing, can indeed vary widely. In my experience, the more positive mindset I have going into an editing sitting, the likelier it is that I will be able to relatively quickly discern which of my photographs deserve to be saved and edited and which I without too much hesitation can cast away.

My rationale for keeping or alternatively removing images from a session is based on a few simple but crucial questions that I ask myself:

Does the image evoke a sense of pride and emotion within me?

If it does not, can it possibly be edited, cropped or retouched to make it worth keeping?

What is my current state of mind? If I'm feeling unsure, should I keep it and decide at a later date?

There have been many occasions over the years when I, in retrospect, realize that I have been hypercritical and later regretted having made choices about deleting images too rashly.

I have always felt a certain level of anxiety or apprehension about permanently deleting my digital photographs, especially penile images. I

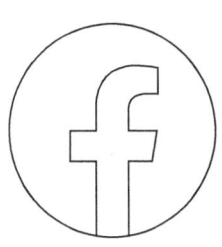

honestly don't remember if I felt similarly cautious or hesitant when I was photographing with analog film. But I do still maintain a sizable collection of prints from those early days of my obsession with penile photography and will likely not discard any of these now vintage images that remain in my cabinet.

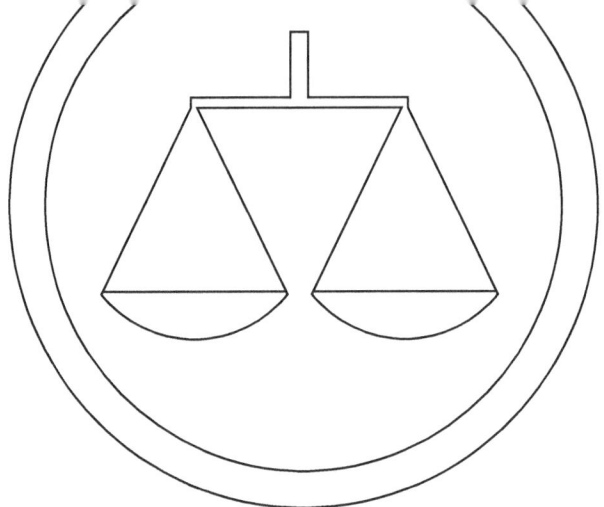

Protecting Intellectual Rights for Penile Photographers

According to the US Federal Copyright Act of 1976, all photographs are protected by copyright from the very moment of creation.

Below is the U.S. Copyright Office outline for these laws. Which are by no means worth anything in other countries, but as the US is home to many of the world's celebrated penile photographers, I find it is very relevant to include it.

"Ownership of a 'copy' of a photograph — the tangible embodiment of the 'work' — is distinct from the 'work' itself — the intangible intellectual property. The owner of the 'work' is generally the photographer or, in certain situations, the employer of the photographer. Even if a person hires a photographer to take pictures of a wedding, for example, the photographer will own the copyright in the photographs unless the copyright in the photographs is transferred, in writing and signed by the copyright owner, to another person. The subject of the photograph generally has nothing to do with the ownership of the copyright in the photograph."

I highly recommend watermarking each of your penile photographs with your name, regardless of whether or not you intend to make them public or distribute online or elsewhere. In addition, there are also many online services, in several countries, available to help copyright and protect your images from illicit or inappropriate usage. A simple online search for "copyright protecting photographs" will provide a wealth of guides, options and venues to pursue.

I have heard of photographers that earn more from pursuing and consequently suing companies and private individuals who have infringed on their copyrighted images then by income generated through direct or indirect sales. You may also have heard of individuals and companies that have been sued for unlawfully using copyrighted images online where steep fines, usually based on the amount of calculated viewers, the value the photographs are assumed to have added, and the length of time illicit publication, have been court ordered.

Exhibiting your penile imagery

In addition to the countless venues where you can publish and exhibit your work online, I also suggest searching for physical galleries and exhibition locations that typically specialize in nude photography. Though perhaps rare in your immediate neighborhood, most larger cities usually have a gallery that would at least consider exhibiting work of this nature. And even if there isn't such a venue near you, don't allow this to hinder you from discovering potentially interesting places where to show your penile images. As long as you are unequivocally honest, upfront and transparent about your intentions and communicate the exhibit's artistic theme publicly – to warn sensitive viewers and age inappropriate visitors – there is really no limit as to where and when you show your work.

My very first solo show consisted of 25 black and white images of my penis at various angles, lighting concepts and phases of engorgement. The exhibit took place early in 2015 in a small gallery located in New York's SoHo district. As a means to show respect to unaware by-passers, I chose to cover the gallery's storefront windows with opaque paper where I had the following text written in beautiful, hand-drawn calligraphy:

"Welcome to The Art of Penile Photography, a series of unique images of the male reproduction organs as seen through the visionary eyes of a photographer."

Below was a disclaimer that clearly communicated the nature of the show.

"This gallery show is intended for a mature audience of adults who can appreciate the effort and creativity involved and enjoy viewing penile photography without prejudice or intolerance."

There were many visitors during the month-long exhibit and though I only sold a total of four images, the gallery owner conveyed to me that most of those that visited the show appreciated my work. In the gallery's guest book there were even several visitors that wrote about how their initial perspectives on the theme had shifted from skeptical to positive and that they were even appeased for being exposed to this new art genre. Such comments are in themselves wonderfully gratifying and fuel my ambition to continue with penile photography.

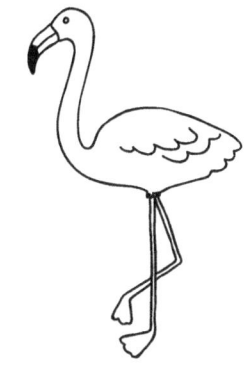

Chapter 9

Spicing things up with creative ideas

This is a chapter dedicated to readers and fellow creatives who desire to expand their visual boundaries beyond what penile photography typically encompasses. The ideas will hopefully inspire traditionalists and modernist alike by expelling how with just a minimum of effort and perhaps a simple prop, it is easy to spice things up. So that they too can breathe a bit of fresh air into their perhaps temporarily stagnant creative universe.

Props and Supportive Accessories

From discussions within the growing penile photography global community, one of the most popular ways to enhance a shooting session is to accessorize it.

Let's get one aspect of this out of the way immediately. For some there is a risk that by accessorizing and spicing things up, one might be tempted to introduce elements of erotic or pornographic nature. In my view, this approach is nothing more than a visual crutch and would not only be unfair towards the artform itself, but would also be completely counterintuitive to my personal outlook and aspiration of elevating penile photography way beyond such a shallow, meaningless perspective. A perspective where a penis and its accompanying scrotum are simply seen as sexual organs and denied any aesthetic value or artistic worth when not engaged as such. I therefore suggest refraining from focusing on easy, quick-fix solutions that will inevitably distract attention and likely derail your objectives.

That's not to say that I am fully against using props that add complexity and implied context. Such is the human experience, we can never fully assume, at any given time or place, to know exactly how people will interpret your creativity. Over the years, I have experienced this most enigmatic conundrum on many occasions. However, in recent times, after attempting to tirelessly fight for the point of view I had so obsessively attempted to make clear and concise, I have chosen to embrace rather than exclude the wide range of conclusions and views my work will inescapably generate. This is the fate of every artist that chooses to publicly exhibit their work.

Small crystals and shiny objects

After extensive experimentation, I've obtained interesting results when using small, round crystals, shiny, asymmetrical gemstones and basically anything that catches and somehow reflects light. Here I include all light sources such as my flash, from a continuous lighting setup, the sun or other ambient light sources.

I would like to underscore here that the amount of accessories that I employ is never excessive or exaggerated. On the contrary, I find the best results are generally achieved with a minimalistic approach. As previously mentioned in this guide, I attributed much of my creative success as a penile photographer to my ability to refrain from the overstated, lavish application of potentially distracting accessories. While this is a fact, I readily admit that within my process, I begin with a measure of indulgence and then slowly chip away until I've reached a level or an equilibrium that subtly adds additional breadth and depth to my composition.

Regardless of what and how you intend on placing or using accessories, anatomical variations make it entirely impossible to make suggestions that will work for all. Like with much of artistry, I firmly believe that it is beneficial if you allocate time and space, as well as a generous amount of patience for trial and error. Some argue that it is failure, not success, that is the mother of all noteworthy achievements. That only when you've failed, will you fully appreciate the path you must venture on as one full of both practical learning and artistic growth. In essence, don't despair even when you're at the very beginning of a penile photography session are unable to realize or envision a thought or idea on how to use a particular accessory.

Never give up. Keep at it, because, eventually, those trials and failures will generate valuable knowledge to help you move forward.

List of suggestions

Here is my extended list of various miniatures or small-scale objects I have used – with varying degree of creative accomplishment – within the context of my penile imagery:

Miniatures
Hats
Scarfs
Scissors
Toothbrush
Tweezers
Cars
Candy
Chocolate (dark)
Bourbon
Bandaids (color neutral)
Watches (digital and analogue)
London Bridge
Cruise ship

Lego (always blue or red pieces, never yellow or white)
Comb
Crystals
Rubies (fake)
Sawdust
Cornflakes
Rice Crispies
Fruit Loops

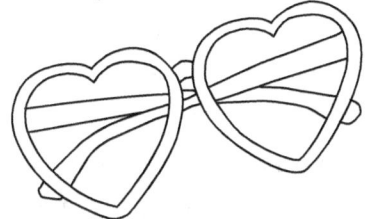

The distance, natural or temporarily induced, between the penis and the scrotum can make for an interesting destination insofar as where to place an accessory before the photography session begins.

Obviously, this puts a demand on whether or not you choose a self-timing or wireless remote shutter release solution, in order to be able to create the composition before it is time to capture it.

The Putty Solution

(What about putty sticking to hair? Ouch) I find that using a non-toxic, adhesive putty can work beautifully in most of these situations, at least where gravity isn't a crucial concern to be reckoned with. For example, if you choose to use a shiny stone or anything with a reflective surface to create a pattern or figure of some kind, using your fingers to roll small balls of adhesive putty, will usually suffice nicely as a means to attach a decorative object to the often rough and uneven skin of your scrotum. I suggest making sure that your scrotum is dry and not cold as this can create a surface that is too lumpy or craggy for even a larger ball of putty to suffice. Likewise, make sure to dry off the shaft, glans or any other place you may choose to add ornamentation on the penis before application. Also, depending of course on placement, please do consider that as the girth of the penis may fluctuate if and when swelling occurs (which it usually does), this may cause the adhesive to lose its sticking properties and cause the object fastened on it to fall off.

Food & Beverages

I am clearly not an advocate of using any kind of food or beverage in my compositions. That's not to say that I haven't seen and at times even admired colleagues that have pursued this path. As mentioned previously, minimalism has been at the forefront of my cultural narrative and it permeates most of my choices and prerogatives. These decisions are often made subconsciously, almost instinctively, without ambiguity or temporization.

Nonetheless, I've seen interesting photos where food and beverages have been juxtaposed with penile images. Mostly concepts with exotic fruits, legumes and herbs. I have even seen images from several photographers inspired by artists like the Italian painter Giuseppe Arcimboldo (1527 – 1593) best known for painting portrait heads by creating them with life-like flowers, fish, fruits, vegetables and books.

One Armenian photographer, who wished to be unnamed in this book, developed several creative ways to make use of cannabis leaves and dried opium poppies to decorate his penile imagery. The earthy hues and organic shapes from these plants produced a beautifully understated palette and composition that allowed the penis and scrotum to take center stage without causing much of a distraction.

I have also experienced a completely different approach where a seemingly serious penile photographer poured molasses or syrup onto his stomach and allowed sufficient time for the flow of the thick liquid to reach and partially cover the base, about an inch up the shaft and most of the scrotum. Though this certainly resulted in a somewhat interesting creation, drops from the scrotum onto the mirror the photographer was sitting on during the session, generated some unwanted reflections that did not serve the final image particularly well. The syrup or molasses was applied so generously, and the time it likely had to take for him to clean up between shots, must have made this particular penile photography session very sticky and lengthy. Similarly, a friend shared with me a note about a Master of Confectionary, working at a famous hotel in Moscow, that covered his entire penis and scrotum (after shaving off his pubic hair) with a blend of three different dark chocolates.

Computer generated accessories (aka CGA)

For those penile photographers proficient in advanced post processing techniques and who have access to applications like Photoshop or Procreate, it is quite common to accessorize by adding decorations afterwards.

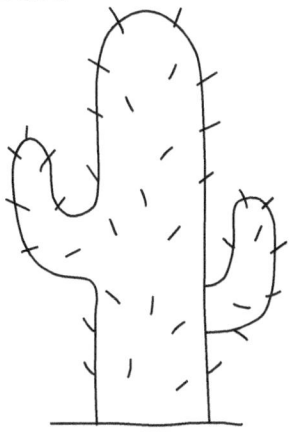

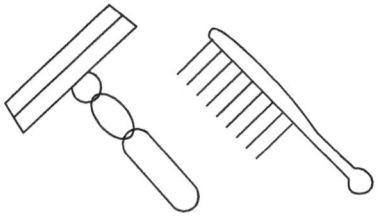

Chapter 10

Manscaping &
Genital Skin Care

First a few words on skin care. Genital grooming is primarily focused on maintenance of the pubic hair. Skin care with moisturizers and other dermatological lotions are also important for genital health and optimum photography results. I strive for the characteristic "healthy glow" which is relatively easily obtained by proper hydration of the skin without inadvertently generating unwanted reflective spots or wider regions on or next to the scrotum, shaft or penis head. With "glow" in this context, I am referring to a radiant shine that enhances rather than distracts the viewer from their artistic objective.

A dry penis and scrotum is not beautiful, and even the best photographic conditions will be unable to camouflage an aura of hygienic neglect that characterizes uncared for genitalia. Whenever you plan a penile photography shoot, I strongly recommend applying a regime of moisturizers at least three consecutive days in advance. Fortunately, my experience is that even the less expensive facial moisturizing creams and body lotions are well-suited for moisturizing the entire anatomy of the penis and scrotum. Buying more expensive or brand name lotions are, in this regard, like mixing an expensive whiskey with a soft drink – an unnecessary and wasteful way to drink good whiskey. This said, I do advise on being cautious about the cheapest products. It is advisable to take note of the type of chemicals and their concentration that form the foundation of any lotion you intend to apply on your skin. Please note that using potions with high percentages of alcohol or ethanol are not at all suitable unless they also contain a reasonable amount of moisturizing glycerin.

Prior to one particular penile photography session where I had tested a very dense skin cream from a leading manufacturer, and because I was lulled into feeling safe and secure by this skin cream's famous brand name, I was entirely unconcerned about any possible negative side-effects. After applying the first of a three day groundwork treatment on my penis and scrotum, I woke the first morning to find during an inspection that the skin on my penis head was unevenly colored pinkish red and most of the shaft had developed a peculiarly rough texture. Though the irritation was bearable and did not cause much pain or too much discomfort, the color shifts did demand that I postpone the intended penile photoshoot for about a week.

Taking Care of The Big 3

Regardless of your compositional goals and theme, I strongly recommend that you always consider these three specific manscaping areas when aiming to achieve the best possible aesthetic results; back, sack, and crack.

Of course, personal preferences differ. Over the years, I have met several serious penile photographers in multiple countries and cultures that prefer composing with longer, thicker and even unruly hair in the pubis region. They uniformly argue that this allows for considerably more flexibility. Though I personally prefer shooting with shorter, more tidy bushiness, which again may be an inherited aesthetic value, I can still appreciate the potential molding properties longer, thicker pubic hair will inherently provide.

Among younger, dark-haired men, pubic hair tends to be darker, thicker and more lively. Blondes and fair-skinned men, as well as older gentlemen, will typically have lighter and often thinner hair. For most men, regardless of age, skin or hair type, growth begins around the naval and extends all the way down to the very base of the shaft, under and surrounding the scrotum as well as on all sides of the anus, the buttocks's crevice and commonly further up towards the lower back region.

While cleaning up unwanted elements in your composition can certainly be accomplished in Photoshop or other image editing software, spending adequate time preparing for a penile photo shoot, will provide more time for creative decisions (as opposed to removing debris).

The most important advice I can provide in this final chapter and to end this book with is to experiment. Only through experimentation and by challenging yourself will you be able to evolve and grow your creativity. Free your mind and your penile photography will follow.